JUDY RENTZ

FIGHTING
to
SURVIVE

My nightmare of Pudendal Nerve and Entrapment

ExplOra
BOOKS

EXPLORA BOOKS
700 – 838 West Hastings St. Vancouver, BC V6C 0A6
www.explorabooks.com
Phone: (604) 330 6795

ISBN: 978-1-998394-36-4 (Paperback)
978-1-998394-12-8 (eBook)

Fighting to SURVIVE

My Nightmare of Pudendal Nerve Entrapment

JUDY V RENTZ

Dedication

I write this only to give
honor and praise to God my Savior Jesus!
For the provision of doctors who have saved my life!
Praying others suffering this nightmare might find
hope, strength and the will to fight on by reading this
humble offering.

Judy Rentz

Table of Contents

FIGHTING
to
SURVIVE
My nightmare of Pudendal Nerve and Entrapment

CHAPTER 1

A Lifetime of Pain

I had known pain almost my entire life, at least as long as I could remember from the age of four. I was a home-delivered (by a country doctor), ten-pound breech baby, badly handled and pulled and tugged! My mother was surely dying after a full day of labor and having delivered eight previous siblings. My older sisters remember it as a day of extreme horror! My mother would tell me as a child growing up, hurting of hip and leg pain, many times that she never dreamed I would be born alive.

I have delivered two babies with practically no anesthesia or blocks. Since the age of twenty-five, I have suffered with very serious fibromyalgia pain, long before the disease was "in vogue" and was hastily given a fibro diagnosis for muscle and joint pain. Nothing could have prepared me for unrelenting and horrific pain that began in June 2007.

Discovering a Passion for Gardening

While in Pittsburgh in 1995, I discovered the thing I had so much passion about was gardening, landscape and design. Mostly self-taught at that time, I began to install a one-half acre strolling garden. Along its pathway, I would create and build structures I thought necessary to enhance my outdoor living for the five months of warm weather that comes to Pittsburgh. I had become quite a "Martha Stewart," completing a pergola, play houses, back drops and trellises and numerous plant-specific gardens. Many joyful hours were spent with my new granddaughter, teaching her to love nature, communing with nature and God. I soon began planning and landscaping friend's yards and tackling church grounds, senior's homes and community properties in our town of Butler Pennsylvania. My body undertook projects worthy of a lawn team. But this type of hard work was nothing unusual for me. I decided to study gardening at the Penn State campus in Pittsburgh. I dove in, studying master gardening with analytical zeal.

Retirement and Remodeling

At that time, my husband, Ben, and I had just found our retirement home in Tennessee, outside of Knoxville near my birthplace. It was nothing extravagant or large since we had planned to be there very little as we would finally be able to hop all over the country, seeing places that time, work, family, and money had prohibited. We kept our home in Pittsburgh close to where our two granddaughters were living. The plan was to travel back and forth until Ben finally retired in two years.

In the meantime, I took on the job of remodeling our new, small home in Tennessee. I was capable of this since, for many years I had been a property manager in Atlanta, and over the years had taught myself to be most proficient, completing projects with my own set of tools and knowledge. For one year, I went full force sunup to sundown, full of vigor, accomplishing my goal. I loved physical work and had always done so energetically as I definitely grew up a country girl. So, tackling my new small yard in Tennessee with fanatical zeal presented no obstacles. It went from nothing but oak trees and poison ivy to my little green haven of beauty and rest! After one year I was able to lounge and do projects for my neighbors and friends. Despite pains I had learned to live with my entire life, I was an energetic, joyful and accomplished woman. Life was good and beautiful.

The Onset of Debilitating Pain

My last venture in June of 2007 was my neighbor's yard. With strong men to do the labor, (I couldn't resist the dirt though) I found myself having to go home and lie down with dull low backaches. I would rest for awhile and be back up and "at 'em." I thrive on accomplishing a project, but after about four weeks of worsening pain, constantly having to rest, I saw my primary doctor. She tried some light pain medication and muscle relaxers with no positive effect. I just had more pain! After a month, she referred me to one of the top orthopedic specialists and surgeons at the University of Tennessee Medical Center in Knoxville. He, of course, prescribed more medication and physical therapy for months. Still with worsening pain and no medication that seemed to help, I headed back to the most highly recommended doctors. Going the short distance to see him had been so painful, feeling every bump in the road. I had held onto the wall slowly making my way back to his office! After asking how I was and my answer of "just terrible," he quickly snapped that he couldn't help me! Now I am tough and don't cry easily, but after many weeks of pain becoming worse, I broke and crumbled to the floor, asking him how I was supposed to live? He hatefully answered walking out the door, "See a psychiatrist!" All this happened in less than 5 minutes. I wept uncontrollably. What in the world am I going to do? This pain was not in my head and I did not need mental help. Sadly, many sufferers get the same recommended advice. So, this is what I live with!

The Progression of Fibromyalgia

By fall of 2007, still thinking I only had a disc problem, my fibromyalgia set in with the coming of cool weather. The back pain kept getting more severe, along with the persistent pressure of spinal pain, sacrum pain, and the pressure of muscles in my pelvic region with rectal spasms and coccyx pain. My life had already come to a grinding halt as I stopped every volunteer project and my landscaping business just to keep my body at a bearable level of pain.

Referred by my primary doctor to specialists, I had so many x-rays, MRIs and neurological exams that my life seemed to consist of nothing but doctors' visits. Of course, I was given many pain relievers, always letting my doctors know that I had thrown away the previous ones since absolutely nothing would touch my pain. I was constantly lying down, writhing and thinking I was in the worst condition I could possibly get. The two things I vowed and determined to do was stay in my church one hour a week and go to choir rehearsal. These became my lifeline, and I swore not to wear this disease on my face. I have sung, I think since the womb, and choir was one way, even though I always hurt, to distract my mind somewhat from what was going on inside my body. Quickly and surely, my belief that whatever this monster was could not become worse was dashed away. Sitting and standing were just intolerable.

My mind was in a constant state of prayer as my normally happy and upbeat spirit turned to a constant state of weeping and "whys?" Crying had not been easy for me, but as every minute of the day was consumed by excruciating pain, my heart and mind gave way to begging God for help, waking every morning believing the pain would subside, but gradually, realizing it was creeping up my body as surely as the sun kept rising.

A Glimmer of Hope

On one such Sunday morning as I willed myself to get out of bed, get some coffee, and try to eat (you see pain overrides any hunger) I made my way the few miles to church. (Ben was still in Pittsburgh at this point.) I struggled to make it through the service, unable to concentrate on what was sung or said and too timid to let even a friend next to me know what dire condition I was in. One must stay strong, especially when no doctor can say what is wrong. Crying, I slowly crept out into a now empty hallway. My pastor, Dr. Jerry Russell, spotted me. I am so thankful that he sensed and saw my agony on my face. I immediately broke down and he led me into his office. I went on to tell him my saga, how I had suffered for months, had lain in agony, but no doctor had a diagnosis. I wept uncontrollably, feeling no professional had helped me or would ever help me.

I told him of my experience with the prestigious ortho. He quickly let me know he had also slammed the door to that same doctor's office! That was sweet music to my ears! He had used a different, well-known orthopedic surgeon and highly respected specialist. He proceeded to let me know he would get a speedy appointment with his back specialist. "If he can't help you, he will send you on to someone who can." I left, blessed and went to my bed knowing help would come. I had been so hesitant to let anyone in on my misery. He called soon to let me know young Dr. Kilifer at University of Tennessee Medical Center would see me. At last, someone would care.

CHAPTER 2

The Search for Relief

During all this time my husband was trying to finish his last year at JC Penney Co. in Pittsburgh. I had managed some trips back, but by Thanksgiving of 2008 it was evident that my driving days were gone. I had arrived at that Thanksgiving in so much pain that I could only lie flat for 10 days. We did manage to take our 6-year-old granddaughter to see the display windows in a grand, old downtown Pittsburgh department store. That was a sweet respite of joy. Ben would come to Tennessee more often, and not once did I ask him to stay. His life was full with his career, much activity, many people, and our daughter's family to enjoy. Thankfully I had a close friend at church who would come if anything at our Tennessee home needed a man's hand.

The Diagnosis

By late fall of 2008, I had once again started the grueling process of medical appointments, scans, MRIs, test after test with my new orthopedic doctor and other specialists to rule out other possibilities that could cause my awful pain. Finally, I met back with my orthopedic doctor expecting a diagnosis and a course of action. He, so sadly, told me he couldn't help.

I saw the pain on his face as he said nothing could be done surgically. "He said, "I would put bolts and concrete in you if it would help." Another spinal diagnosis that so very many of us suffering get. But I stayed strong. My pastor had said he would surely refer me on to another doctor who would know what to do. Almost as an afterthought he said he wanted me to see a physiatrist. A what? I knew what a psychiatrist was but had never heard of this field of medicine. I learned that Knoxville Tennessee had been graced with five of these elite physicians who knew every nerve, fiber, tendon and muscle of the human body. But still another specialist! I toyed with the idea of not even going. Ben was the voice of reason, "What did I have to lose?" I saw Dr. Donald Lakatosh immediately. This would bring the first clue of what my problem was, after over a year of endless appointments, high hopes and hopeless disappointments.

The Pudendal Nerve

This brilliant doctor read the referral and briefly questioned me. Then he had me walk down a hallway in front of him. Very matter of fact, he touched the side of my left hip which had hurt my entire life and said, "I know what's wrong with you, pudendal nerve damage." This was the first time I had heard this word! Now you may ask, "What is a pudendal nerve?" as I did.

Many, many thousands of hurting people, and many doctors have never heard the word pudendal. There are so few in the United States, they can be counted on one hand, and presently there are only two highly recommended specialists and surgeons. France has just lost their only specialist, leaving only a few who even know the disease in Europe, but do not practice treating it!

"The pudendal nerve is a sensory, autonomic, and motor nerve that carries signals to and from the genitals, anal area and urethra. There are slight differences in the nerve branches for each person, but typically three branches of the pudendal nerve on each side of the body, the rectal branch, a perineal branch and a clitoral/penile branch. The anatomy of the pudendal nerve is extremely complicating leaving only specialist to understand and non-medically trained, as myself, trying to explain as I do when asked. I do understand that the nerves are symmetrical on each side of the lower spine, weaving itself through and around the pelvic area, coming down from the sacral nerve, traveling through the muscle around tendons and ligaments. An extreme pudendal neuralgia entrapment, interrupts sexual sensations, bladder and bowel function, creating a myriad of pain signals."

The Treatment

Dr. D. Lakatosh contacted a colleague, Dr. E. Pinzon who I quickly saw. He is an orthopedic pain specialist. The two doctors studied me, sometimes even calling to see if I had been able to sleep. Now somewhere in my visits to and from the two doctors, the word pudendal nerve was never mentioned again. Dr. Pinzon diligently started pain relief for coccydynia, a condition of broken, bruised or inflamed coccyx. These procedures were done under anesthesia and numbing anti-inflammatory meds as much as could be given and direct blocks into the ganglion of the spine. This is an encapsulated area at the tail bone where nerves meet going into the spinal column and to the brain. I truly believe the blocks and ablations were effective at times, never lasting long enough, but, I gladly repeated the procedure's many, many times until my pain became more widespread and severe. I must say that Dr. Pinzon was so compassionate and studied any procedure he thought would benefit.

The problem was just not my coccyx.

I was once again flat in bed, gritting and flailing as every muscle stab and tear gripped me! During this time, I was referred to a highly recommended physical therapist in Knoxville. I had my doubts at hearing physical therapist again, but I learned she was not ordinary. She only worked on cases of the most damaged and baffling, painful referrals, people who had been crushed, men who had fallen on girders and beams and sufferers like me who had no other avenue of help. I contacted her, learning she was booked for many months. Ben was in Tennessee at this time for a brief stay and took the phone from me. I heard him on the phone, "You don't understand, she is in horrendous pain, can't sit, can't stand, and it has been for over a year!" This truly was a busy physical therapist. The appointment would have to be in eight months. Ben gave up pleading and said he would get back with them. But, evidently the receptionist had relayed my information to Donna Edwards. She called back immediately and saw me the next day, plus three times a week for eight months. I never knew of internal physical therapy, but the pudendal nerve and levator ani muscle stretches across the pelvic floor, in my case, tearing from side to side. It was the most excruciating process, done vaginally, and anal muscles were stretched and manipulated trying to correct the inward bending of my coccyx. It was a dreaded process, comparable to the pain of childbirth. There was nothing to do but hang on, moan, cry and grit my teeth. The therapy was excruciating, but what could I do except endure? However, I began to have a little ease of pain in my pelvic and tailbone area. After eight months of three weekly visits, my pain did lessen, enabling me to walk somewhat better for about two months. The relief was short-lived and walking soon became impossible yet again.

CHAPTER 3

Finding Hope in Faith

I truly believe God had sent help in the provision of compassionate doctors. They tried every avenue to ease my pain, but I begged my Father, God to send help! It was my constant prayer, "Oh God please send help, oh God ease this pain!" I knew I was the object of his love, but how could he see me weeping, begging for healing mercy? How could he want this for me?"

I haven't described the pain of the torment going on in my body. The only way to describe this monster is to say I was in a constant state of labor with the crowning sensation of having a baby and feeling as if my tail bone was constantly being physically torn from my body! I experienced continuous rectal spasms, jabbing muscle pains and continual pelvic pressure. Also, the pain began to radiate to my sacrum and the entire lower torso. This pain never ceased. I was blessed in that I had a medication to sleep, since I had become an insomniac at age 35. This sleep was the only respite and never for very long.

Questioning "Why Me?"

What had I done to deserve this? In such pain, it was so difficult not to question, "Why me?" I had hurt most of my life remembering back to age four, with what doctors' thought was sciatica, onset of serious fibromyalgia at age 25, which is a familial disease and rampant in my large family. With this disease my body ached, and muscles tore as with constant flu. My life in Pittsburgh for 21 years was to leave my bed, straight to an indoor hot tub and directly back inside to an electric blanket. The first onset of the cool weather brought with it the severity of fibromyalgia. Along with this comes debilitating fatigue at intervals. I was totally incapacitated with this onset, too weak to get up for water or even a saltine. Wasn't this enough God?

As I have said, I had found our perfect retirement home in Tennessee, outside of Knoxville, which is where I grew up. Ben needed to work two more years for full retirement benefits. We had planned to keep our Pittsburgh home and travel back and forth. He had informed his superiors that he might have to leave at anytime as I was mysteriously ill. I would never have asked him to make the final move until retirement. He had been so blessed and worked so hard to achieve the corporate job he had. He loved his work dearly.

Seeking Relief in the Emergency Room

The catalyst came one Sunday after church. I still made it there, my refuge. I was home, unable to bear the pain any longer. There was nothing I could do except call the after-hours clinic at my primary doctor's office. Unable to barely speak, I finally got a nurse and tried to explain my condition. Hatefully, she said I could come and stand around the building with the other 100 people with the flu! No pain medicine I had been given eased the symptoms. I tried so hard to bear the horrific pain but decided I had to go to the emergency room at the local hospital, Blount Memorial. A young male doctor saw me. I begged for any relief. After I explained my symptoms, I was given some injections which gave about 10 minutes of pain relief. Weeping, I asked if he could just admit me and let me get some sleep and relief. He agreed, promising he could do that. I had no idea what was to come! I signed his permission paper. I was unaware what the fourth floor was, the psych and drug addiction floor! Everything I had was taken from me, purse, 800mg ibuprofen and migraine medication. I was put in a double room, still innocent by thinking the doctor and nurses would help me. The night turned into total horror. After hours and going across from my room to the nurse's station I still didn't realize what was happening. I was totally ignored each time I begged for help. They stared through me as though I wasn't there! I saw the young doctor pass by several times finally yelling at him, "Why won't you look at me or answer, you lied to me!" It was probably 11:30 PM. They basically close shop for the night as I was pleading for just my ibuprofen. By then I had a massive migraine, as I always get in enclosed spaces. The nurses wouldn't look at me as I wept and held onto their wall. I dragged myself back to my room, helpless. Sometime by early morning, I was going into shock tremors from pain and dry heaving from the migraine. Weeping, pleading for help, I lay on the tile bathroom floor. They didn't seem to know or care that one can suffer a stroke during this severe pain. I only lay on the cold floor begging and praying to die.

The Nightmare in the Hospital

Finally, the other patient in the room with me alerted the nurses of my condition. They came to the bathroom where I lay in agony. They looked at me and told me I had to get into bed all the while as I begged for help. They finally went to my confiscated purse and gave me the ibuprofen which did absolutely nothing to help the nausea producing migraine. The following morning after that tortuous night, I was forced to a hall to do art and activities with the other "inmates." Aggravated and in great pain, I left and was forced to meet with the head psychiatrist. He repeatedly battered me, informing me I was just a drug addict. Enough, I tore into him, informing him he had never had a baby and couldn't fathom my ripping pain. Smirking at me, repeating I was just an addict and I would be back as I left, slamming the door. I informed a nurse I was leaving and demanded they let me call my sister to pick me up who quickly called Ben. He called, surprisingly, they let me speak to him, telling him of my nightmare. He then gave them a tongue lashing. By now a supervisor of the floor was there to convince me to stay. She got the entire story as I shook from anger and cried from pain. Apologetically, she understood why I was leaving, promising to check out my allegations, sure she would! The sad thing is that my primary care doctor was doing rounds on the other floors that night. They could have verified my condition with her. I pray they hadn't contacted her and she had dismissed me. My female doctors had never been compassionate, not even researching my condition. This one horrific night has scarred me forever, making it difficult to trust any medical facility. As I write now, I am livid that medical professionals could be so callous. I warn anyone who contacts me, never go to an emergency room. I digress lengthily with this revelation, but sadly it needs to be told. My husband resigned in Pittsburgh and was home with me that day. This was late 2007.

Relentless Pain

Once again, my life was bad, writhing every minute, yes, every minute with relief only if I could sleep. I have never been able to nap so this respite was only a few hours each night. Dr. Pinzon was still doing anything in his power through blocks and neurotomies or ablations trying to ease my pain. I had no medications, even after trying so many, that would alleviate the pain.

I listened, hopefully if anyone suggested any remedy, even going to Lincoln Memorial University of holistic treatment through snow and blizzards several times. Finally, since I never felt hands on my body, I asked the doctor there what he was doing. He snapped, "I'm treating you!" I asked how as he wasn't touching me. Angry now, he said nothing. As I lay on the exam table, I knew this long-distance pursuit for help was doing nothing for my body!

CHAPTER 4

Desperate Measures

In the Tennessee mountains I tried a healer, praying for me, laying hands on me and then convincing me to take home pints of moonshine mixed with black walnut concentrate. I have never had liquor, so I had this concoction, taking swigs twice a day. I wish I could say it was a hoot, but I felt no difference at all!

Month by month I lay in my beautiful garden on a twin cot we had set on a platform under the oaks. I had my fan and music with the electric cords running underground. Also, in 2008 I had a therapy pool designed just for my body, enough for short laps, leg lifts, holding onto each side, and jets to soothe me. Lying there in the warmth was how my days were spent. Sadly, soothing there so many times, I would think of how easy it would be to stay underwater and breathe. I had always heard what an easy death that would be. Looking to the sky, I would rationalize to God that this would be okay with him if I just couldn't bear any more. It truly was a mental struggle not to do so. When one sees no earthly hope, one thinks of a way, anyway, veering head on into another vehicle, sliding off an overpass, or some way to stop the pain. I meditated, studied my Bible repeatedly, searching words for why this was happening to me. Was there any hidden sin I was doing to bring on punishment? Was a sin of my father being revisited upon me? Searching and gleaning scripture, I tried to find some answer for my dilemma, but no plausible explanation came. "God, have I not given you my everything?"

The Cult Experience

My younger neighbor came one day saying she saw me always there praying, crying, still worshiping. She gave me hand written Bible verses of consolation and faith, which I have fervently used. She asked if I would be opposed to going to a healer. I said I would do anything in this world to rid my body of this pain. We set out at 4am one Sunday morning for Charlotte, North Carolina. A spiritual leader she had known recommended the pastor of Morning Star Ministries. We knew nothing of this organization which was a great mistake. That service on Sunday morning was truly one of the strangest things I had ever witnessed. People were randomly dancing, chanting, painting artwork as others just roamed about. The so-called minister, who had quickly dismissed me, stood and said very few words, but oddly wrote on a board seven verses from the book of James. Shockingly, I had been studying on these verses for the entire week. I know Satan knows Bible verses also. Dismissed, I told someone I had to come for prayer. Many gathered and prayed over me, demanding that I feel healing. Sorry, I did not. I am a fervent believer in prayer and would never speak ill of anyone, and definitely not of prayer. My friend and I left, not saying anything, but each feeling strangely preyed upon. I lay in the back of the SUV as we went home in silence. The next day I called my son, he was in Talbot seminary, asking if he knew anything of this group in Charlotte. He informed me that it was a cult, and I was not surprised. I googled and learned all the shocking details of Morning Star Ministries. Once again, I say anyone with unrelenting, horrific pain will seek out any possible help.

Finding a Name for the Monster

So again, my life ebbed by in my garden as my body dwindled down to 98 pounds at 5'6". In so much pain, eating is almost impossible. Most of the time, I would force myself to eat something to live, while at the same time begging to die. Also, pudendal neuralgia often stops bowel function, therein another dilemma. Some people may find this hard to believe. There was so much ambiguity in my condition. All the while searching for help, hoping, not finding any, trying to accept there was no way I could live on. Such are the thoughts of thousands as we suffer, finding little or no relief or treatment for this horrific disease we now know as Pudendal Neuralgia or entrapment. Women, men and even children are not spared. It can be brought on by a simple fall, hysterectomy, exercise, bladder repair, childbirth, or as I now know, my own mangled birth. Many search and never know why the onset.

CHAPTER 5

A Glimmer of Hope

It had been three years now into this disease. Ben had been retired, at home with me now for one year. In Knoxville, after seeing an orthopedic surgeon for possible help, I decided I was going to John's Hopkins in Baltimore for removal of my coccyx, or to the pelvic pain unit for any possible procedure. Knowing the coccyx removal would put me into a wheelchair, the possibility of no more pain won over. We both started on the phones and internet searching for anything resembling my symptoms. Of course, I was flat in bed again while Ben did anything necessary for me and our home. That night around midnight, he yelled loudly, "you have got to see this," hurrying to my bed to have me see the results of another search. There was the study written by two doctors in California. Unbelievably, with every symptom I had listed, they called the disease Levator Syndrome. Finally, someone knew the pains I had. There was a name! It had to be my disease!

A Pelvic Pain Specialist

As I said, God opened a door the previous afternoon as I left the orthopedics' office, I spotted a sign for a pelvic pain specialist. I told Ben that I was going in. Dr. Dell's office nurse let me know I was to be back in his office the next day. A friend drove me there, as I was just in no condition to be driving, as all I could do was stand, holding onto the counter. As I headed into his office, I had the printed information we had found the night before on the internet. Dr. Dell's first question to me was did I have any medication. I explained that no drug had touched the pain. I would just toss them when they didn't help. I guess my blood pressure was high and I was shaking severely from pain. He insisted the first order was to find pain medication. I then laid my printed information on his desk and asked, "Do you know this disease?" Yes, I do. I will do an exam to confirm," he said. I warned him that my gynecologist could not touch me during an exam just a few weeks ago. Every touch felt like a knife cutting me, and I had just screamed. Sadly, even though I had a condition so severe the doctor could not examine me, I was sent home with only Miralax for medication. I was given no other suggestions for help at all. Being a pelvic specialist, Dr. Dell knew how to proceed, letting me know he would not do the barbaric test that my husband was so afraid to let me see, fearing I would not see a specialist. He had found the tests used to diagnose Levator Syndrome when he found the symptoms of this disease.

A Name for the Monster

My exam was practically painless, shocking me into saying, "You didn't hurt me." His experience with pain in women proved to be excellent. As he came back to the exam room, he held two prescriptions for stronger medications. Then saying, "Yes you do have Levator Syndrome, but I do not treat it and know of no one in the Southeast who does." As this news should have shattered me, I was elated to have a name for my "monster." Finally, I just knew, I was on my way toward finding help. I left with a lighter heart and hope. He has said later that he would never forget that pitiful, shaking, emaciated woman he saw holding onto the wall as I made my way down the hall and into his office.

Searching for Treatment

Since Ben had given up his career and retired early to care for me, our lives were consumed with searching for answers for the Levator Syndrome disease. We had contacted highly acclaimed university hospitals, asking if they had a pelvic pain treatment facility. Now, one might think the question would have a quick answer. We called all over the United States. Finally, getting the question answered about a treatment facility, I was relayed from one extension to another, sometimes finally getting a "no" or "We'll get back to you." We finally pursued Vanderbilt, Duke, Emory and Johns Hopkins. Getting to the right source to answer required reaching the personal nurse working with the specialist, with repeated calls, transfers and emails. Over three weeks passed without an answer. Driving home from the pelvic pain specialist, Dr. Dell, I went straight to bed. Immediately the phone rang. First, from Duke University, "We don't treat that," from the specialist's nurse. From the other two teaching hospitals, came the same answer. I told myself, "Ok, but we have a name. Surely treatment can be found."

Help Arrives

The next call came from Dr. Chen, head of the pelvic pain department at John Hopkins. She was calling to make sure we did not waste airfare and lodging costs when we arrived in two days if they didn't treat my symptoms. I was ecstatic to tell her we had a name now for the pain, Levator Syndrome. "Oh, but no, we don't treat that!" I reminded her I was still on my way to have my coccyx removed, still believing that it had to help relieve the excruciating pain. She asked me to refresh her memory of my pain. I rattled off each horrible symptom. She told me to stay by the phone, as if I could do anything else. She was finding help for me. The phone rang back in less than 10 minutes. She informed me that I could come to her friend, Dr. Richard Marvel, in Maryland the next day. I also could see a fellow specialist in Chattanooga, Tennessee, Dr. A Nieves. I wept, thanked her profusely, and rang the number for Dr. Nieves, a pelvic pain specialist and reconstructive surgeon. What shocked me so, was that he was located in Chattanooga, just two hours away, and none of the doctors in Knoxville even knew he was nearby to help me.

Finding Hope in Dr. Nieves

At last, praise God! There was help. I talked to his nurse and she was adamant that I should come. She had seen miracles walk out of his office! I was a little skeptical as I had been to homeopaths, chiropractors, orthopedics, holistic and even to Tennessee mountain doctors and healing services. Dr. Nieves's nurse wept as I told her I had been battling this unnamable pain for almost 3 years. It was now April 2010. She told me to be in his office at 11am the next day!

CHAPTER 6

A Sleepless Night of Reflection

That night was sleepless as so many had been. I relived every minute of the past two days. I believe it was no accident that Ben and I saw an office sign for pelvic pain as we left the orthopedics' office preparing me for my trip to John Hopkins to remove my coccyx. It was no accident that Ben had discovered a disease sounding exactly like mine the night before I was to be in Dr. Dell's office. Certainly, it was no accident that all four University hospitals called the same afternoon that my pain was confirmed as Levator Syndrome. It was also no accident that Dr. Nieves, the specialist of this disease was only two hours away in Chattanooga. Help had finally come. My God was big!

The First Appointment with Dr. Nieves

Morning came. I could not get to Chattanooga quickly enough. Someone was going to help me! Dr. Nieves turned out to be the most compassionate doctor I had ever seen. The nurse began the questionnaire and evaluations. I soon got into an exam room, where she began with catheters and blood testing to be sent off to check for bacteria or any abnormality. The bladder is filled with solutions and my reaction was recorded. It was not pleasant at all, with a great deal of painful burning.

This is a condition I have ignored all my life as normal for me, frequent urination and some burning intermittently. There is no cure for interstitial cystitis, damage to the lining of the bladder. The lining doesn't regenerate. There is a very strict diet one can follow and taking Elmiron, which cost thousands of dollars monthly and is not covered by any insurance. My husband, being wise, later googled any other medication discoveries. Elmiron, the prescribed medicine, is synthetic aloe vera. Real aloe vera gel caps are now available at vitamin and herbal shops. I find these as helpful as prescription medications. However, neither bring total relief.

The Internal Blocks

The appointment was quite lengthy. Dr. Nieves and Ben had a long conversation in the corner. I was finished with the nurse and exams. He checked me and let me know he could not do the internal blocks that week but on the next appointment. Of course, I cried and begged, but there was just no room on the surgical schedule. I dressed and moved to the door. The doctor came, and I noticed he had five prescriptions in his hand. I saw what three were, morphine, opium suppositories and oxycodone. I said, "No, No!" My medication never helped the pain. He kept pushing toward me, I, refusing as I was so afraid of narcotics. My husband was angry and assured me that the doctor would help me wean off. I just could not accept them. Dr. Nieves got into my face, waving the prescriptions, "You will not survive this disease without them." I relented and many, many times I have thanked him repeatedly.

We returned to Chattanooga for the internal block treatment on the following Monday. We met in his office exam room before going up to the hospital procedure room. The emotional, compassionate nurse advised me an exam must be done before he moved ahead on the procedure. Tears fell as she told me that this was going to be the most painful thing I had ever gone through. Dr. Nieves had to examine me to locate the areas needing blocks. I let her know I could get through this. She replied with, "No, this will be the most awful thing that'll happen to you." She cried, scared by now, I braced myself. We headed to the exam room. The doctor came in, asking if the nurse had informed me, saying, "this Will be the worst possible thing to go through." I said I would just hold onto the table and pray. The doctor said he would pray also as the poor nurse was still crying in the corner. Now, he wanted me to hold on if I needed to, apologizing, but he had to do this to know what nerves to block. "Are you ready?" he asked as the nurse took my hand, tears rolling. Honestly, I've never known any pain like this as inflamed nerves, tailbone and anal area were touched. This was pain one does not think they will survive. He was trying to finish quickly, but nothing can erase the pain of that exam. I can say with all the gripping pain I have faced I have had no pain like this. He examined me vaginally, horrific as I clung to the table, kicking and screaming and bearing pain much worse than childbirth! I include this, graphically, because it is only one of so many procedures we sufferers go through as research, seeking treatment. I can attest to what I've heard from others concerning nerve pain. At the time, one thinks they can surely not survive! Blessedly, we moved on for the procedure, under anesthesia. I received as many as 60-90 internal injections. Precious, indescribable, relief, sometimes lasting up to 9 months. Dr. Nieves was one of my specialists, who truly saved my life. I am forever indebted and thank God always for His provision.

CHAPTER 7

Returning to Normalcy

With the blocks and medication, my life became reasonably normal. Once again, I could do my beloved landscape design, but not performing the labor. Ben and I could take trips with my pain cooperating. Of course, I have my "big drugs." I was so careful to use them sparingly, terrified of becoming addicted. I weaned myself off after eight months. I was so thrilled to tell Dr. Nieves, surprising him, since I still had great pain, but not deathly pain with the help of internal blocks. Life was good for about 20 months. My visits to Chattanooga for blocks became as frequent as possibly allowed. Several times between blocks, I would have to call, praying he was in town to get smaller treatments in between. Once, I was so desperate, I cut short a week's stay in the mountains with my sister while she raced me to Chattanooga. Meeting Dr. Nieves in his office, I took as many blocks as I could bear with no anesthesia.

The Constant Battle with Insurance

Every return trip to Chattanooga meant there would be a battle with my insurance company. There was only one available insurance for me when Ben retired. Since I had fibromyalgia for so many years, no other companies would cover me. As I said before, this diagnosis has been given so freely, insurance companies decided it was too expensive to cover. I have to be thankful for the one company that accepted me, although the premiums were totally and astronomically expensive each month. My treatments at the "out of network" hospital, University of Tennessee Erlanger Medical Center in Chattanooga began at $7,000 each visit. The kind doctors fee was only $175. With Ben battling representatives at the company, the cost was lowered to $4000 each time. We had to decide if we lost our home for me to live, we would do it.

I had battled with the public relations manager at the insurance company, that if I had cancer, that disease treatment would be covered. And yet, this disease was killing me and would not be covered. So many times, in the first year of treatment, we would receive a prior authorization, then would receive a call that insurance was just not going to cover treatment this time. This is after Ben had the hospital agree to reducing the cost to $4000 each visit. Many times, we would arrive at Erlanger, battling insurance as we walked in. Dr. Nieves had to wait hours as we fought to have parts of the procedure covered. At times, Ben and the doctor would each be on his own phone trying to justify the internal blocks.

This took such a financial and stressful toll on both of us, that we both looked for many ways of coverage short of selling our home or using all the retirement funds. One such day, I decided I had to beg someone in charge at Humana in Lexington, Kentucky. During one of the previous battles, the approval nurse, who I had gotten to know well, frustrated also, gave the name of the CEO of the company. Here comes another God story!

A Desperate Plea to the Insurance CEO

Not knowing what else to do, I got a simple legal pad and poured my heart out. Beginning with, "I'm writing this in plain terms as if I was your wife or mother." It was an eight-page letter, stating most of the gory and embarrassing facts of my battle. I had to make him understand the torture and to place his loved one in my situation. I mailed the letter in a manila envelope, priority mail, to be signed for by the CEO, praying this would accomplish something or anything to alleviate the constant battles of authorization with each of my visits to Chattanooga.

Later, I informed the authorization nurse at Humana what I had done. "Oh no, he will never get the letter if it's to be signed for. There is no chance!" I was told he may have the letter in general mail. All incoming mail was put in a huge bin and sorted eventually. Oh my, I guessed that was the end of that idea. I had sent this lengthy plea from my post office on Friday. On the following Monday, I made another trip to Erlanger for the costly, but priceless blocks procedure. It proceeded as usual with us handing over that astronomical amount for one treatment. On Friday of that week, Ben came to the bedroom, where I always lay, with a strange look on his face, "You won't believe this!" Excited, Ben started reading, "after reading your letter, you can consider any procedure in the future approved and covered." Along with apologies for the trouble before and condolences for my disease and well wishes from the CEO of Humana Insurance.

Somehow, my letter from a huge, truck-size bin, usually taking months to empty had reached him. I choose to believe angels intervened. Once again, a story, all true, reached the proper person who was evidently compassionate. God touching his heart, my prayer had been answered. My God is big and faithful to me!

CHAPTER 8

The Failure of the Nerve Blocks

My trips to Dr. Nieves in Chattanooga were frequent, giving relief so I could function, never with heavy activity, but affording the luxury of existing once again! However, in early 2013, the internal blocks provided only a couple of weeks of pain relief. This is common as pudendal nerve disease progresses. The blocks became a futile attempt at pain relief.

By September of 2013, after a month away from Tennessee, I returned home, once again in desperate need of medical help and attention! I lay day after day in my garden, in and out of my therapy pool. Confessing, so many times that if I just breathed under water the pain would be gone. I constantly prayed and did battle with God, trying to understand the "why" and unable to accept why healing would not come! I will say that these many months brought me to a more intimate closeness to God than I had ever known, despite the battle. Once again, I was calling any surgeon or specialist that might rescue me. No, there was never anyone who even knew the disease! Once, I asked my husband if he would be okay if I just could not live on. He yelled, "That's not an option!" Leaving me in my outside room, asking myself how I could possibly live on.

Finding a Pioneering Surgeon

During the year before, I communicated with sufferers in Europe, repeatedly gleaning any knowledge of the disease. I began to hear news of one surgeon in France, Dr. Robert. He created the surgery for pudendal nerve entrapment but was now retired. After many months of research and realizing there was going to be no help for me, I lay in my garden in September 2013 and put out an internet plea, possibly to any site in Europe or anyone who had knowledge of "the monster!" In desperation, I lay begging to die! In less than 5 minutes, a message came in on my email. It was from Dr. Stanley Antolak in Minneapolis, St Paul. He listed three surgeons in the U.S. and humbly, himself last. I marvel still as to how he happened to see my plea. I owe it to God! The doctor was the pioneer of the pudendal entrapment surgery in the United States, beginning after retiring as a urologist from the Mayo clinic in Minnesota. He had studied the surgery in France under Dr. Robert, who left urology to create the procedure! God had once again sent help!

Dr. Antolak moved as quickly as possible and performed my pudendal nerve entrapment surgery in Minnesota in December 2013. I weighed only 90 pounds, unable to eat, and I know I would not have survived long! The surgery was over 5 hours, performed bilaterally though the hips. Afterwards, the surgical account was of nothing he had ever seen. My pudendal nerve was bound on my left side into something resembling a rubber band ball, covered in a strange cotton-Styrofoam like substance and the right nerve was wrapped around my iliac bone (the large fan-shaped bone) stretched like dental floss, then connecting to my spine! I had zero pain upon awakening and never experienced pain except for pin pricks as the nerves "awoke" weeks later! Dr. Antolak, the kindest, most compassionate doctor I have ever known continues to be my earthly savior, as I have told him. Also telling him that Jesus is my Savior, he could only say "I'm humbled." We continue to talk and share information as he continues to teach throughout the nations!

Retiring in October 2020, I'm sure he will be missed. Also, selfishly we need surgeons. He had paid his dues, one of the four surgeons, and teaching across the world. How precious he is!

Life in Venice, Florida

We were blessed to be able to move to Venice Florida in 2015. What a joy. I actually thought I would be able to enjoy this wonderful town. I was able to stroll a few times. I only walked the beach four times, limited by shifting sand.

I began the search for doctors immediately, as I needed to have prescriptions of antispasmodic and low-grade pain medicine, being oxycodone or Tylenol PM. This along with 800mg ibuprofen had thankfully eased the spasms and deep bone pain in my lower torso, that began every morning around 20 minutes after I awoke. Every day! Those 20 minutes were my respite! I strolled my beautifully landscaped yard and all the southern flowers and shrubs a helper had planted for me. It was alright for me to use a hand shovel and put in small plants, never squatting or bending low, according to Dr. Antolak. This was the only physical activity I was able to do. The very few times I was able to stroll downtown Venice were greatly treasured. And, I still was able to get to church on Sundays, with my special sitting cushion and medication.

The Search for a Primary Care Doctor

Finding a primary care doctor became a seemingly impossible venture. Every day calling, searching for hours, my husband on the computer and phone with me, call after call. If the doctor was accepting new patients, the minute I mentioned pudendal nerve disease, which none, honestly had ever heard of and the fact that I must use the two narcotics, I was told "No, we can't accept you!" For five months, days were consumed by the hunt. Thankfully, fibromyalgia which had kept me bedfast in the north, had miraculously been healed by lying, not in the sun, but in the warmth on my lanai, Praise God!

Finding a Reluctant Doctor

I was becoming desperate, not because I was an addict; I had weaned off many narcotics but knowing I would not be able to handle the pain of pudendal neuralgia! The search ended when I found a nearby walk-in clinic. The only doctor was very hesitant when I said I must keep Oxy-Tylenol 5mg and Clonazepam 5 mg. These are such low-grade controlled drugs. Anyone who has true pain knows they aren't effective on anything more than a toothache! But, I begged! Sad, but true. Of course, he had never heard of the pudendal nerve, but did glance through my records of surgeries and many, many procedures. He finally gave in but would only write a prescription for 10 pills per month. I accepted!

Living with Constant Pain

Once again, since June 2007, my life was lived out in bed. I definitely am not a TV watching person. I would meander through my house, doing what little I could and stroll through my garden. I'm so thankful God gave me a love of nature. It truly was the only thing I could see, meditate and find joy in! I did these little activities for fear of my legs atrophying. I had been such an over-active person, and for years Ben and I had walked 4 miles every day. Thankfully, there is no winter in deep south Florida. So, I was always able to at least have this bit of exercise. But by May of 2016, my pain had become constant and greatly increased. I had found a primary care doctor, older and ready to retire who had heard of pudendal nerve entrapment, but only as a "biker's disease." I had asked for the most compassionate doctor in the group. He certainly was that!

Seeking Pain Management Solutions

The disease progressed, and he was willing to increase my pain medication to 7.5 mg Oxycodone that with the 5 mg Clonazepam helped, but no drug ever eased the pain in my coccyx and anal area. So many sufferers must fight constipation. The pudendal nerve disease interrupt's function and so many patients die of sepsis. The elimination process becomes impossible. The other leading cause of death is suicide. Pudendal entrapment neuralgia is often referred to as "the suicide disease." Eventually, the human mind and body cannot bear the pain! Remember, there are hundreds of thousands of sufferers. Many never knowing what the disease is since even medical students are not taught the condition.

Finding a Compassionate Specialist

My greater pain began. I had never heard of an interventional radiologist but, by googling, I learned that it was also a pain management field. I started contacting many of these specialists but continued to be rejected as a patient. I called the local hospital and RAVE was recommended (Radiological Associates of Venice). At first, the nurses had never heard of the disease, and the doctor did not treat it. But, with rising pain, I begged the nurses to watch my video on YouTube that I had done before the 2013 surgery. They begged Dr. Craig Reiheld to take me as a patient. I saw him immediately. He is so kind and tries so hard to alleviate pain. He wanted to know everything and admitted he had never heard the word pudendal. But he saw my pain, studied, got equipment from Germany and began months of many blocks, trying to find what and where blocks were most effective. At times, I was scared there would be a time when nothing could be done. He promised me there would always be something for me. He saw me after attacks and researched more for any procedure to be done! So compassionate, he is one of my angels!

The Agony of Pudendal Nerve Attacks

The pain of an attack is hard to explain. Internal pain gets stronger and starts to radiate in every direction of the body. Increasingly, the tail bone and surrounding muscles feel as though they are literally being pulled out. In the first 6 ½ years of this disease I had the sensation of labor contractions and crowning of a baby. This pain became stronger as the tail bone pressure grew. My body began to shake uncontrollably as an inner quivering of seemingly all internal nerves took over to the top of my head. In the past, these were not short episodes, as I held onto bedposts, rolled in the bathroom floor, begging God to please let me die. After taking enough of my pain medication, previously given I would eventually calm. These were opium suppositories, morphine, boluses and oxycodone. Six months after the surgery in 2013 when the pain returned, Dr. Antolak concocted a prescription for a suppository with Clonidine, Diazepam, Bupivacaine, and Gabapentin. Thankfully, my primary doctor in Tennessee, Nils Gaddis, had agreed to prescribe these after he agreed to work with Dr. Antolak on my aftercare. I have been so blessed with compassionate male doctors. Tears fell as he had read through my stack of medical records. I finally had a primary doctor who really cared.

Stranded During an Attack

When we first moved to Florida, I had none of these suppositories left, due to not yet having found a doctor to prescribe them. One Saturday afternoon that summer, I felt I could gently stroll downtown. I was having a very good day, and suddenly an attack swept through me. I had just been to the interventional radiologist about two weeks before. Knowing I couldn't drive home and thinking I had to call an ambulance, I called the RAVE center. Thankfully, I was able to talk to a nurse, filled her in on what was happening and that I was stranded downtown. Telling me to hold on, she moved mountains to get the rectal suppository prescription. Doctor Reiheld was at his family home in North Carolina. The nurse searched for a doctor, finding one that was kind enough to approve the medication. I finally did make it to my home and my husband had picked up the prescription. I will be eternally grateful to her and the kind mystery doctor. They believed the pain! So many medical professionals have told myself and so many others, "See a psychiatrist." This was just one of so many horrible events! So many pudendal nerve sufferers have bluntly been told the same. We fight to make the medical professionals believe our horrendous pain is Real!

Living with Unimaginable Pain

I lived on, chronic, crippling unimaginable pain. I have much to live for, six precious grandchildren, two great kids, compassionate and giving husband, a devoted life to Christ in which I long to do mission work. But, it is difficult at times to accept knowing that tomorrow will be just like today – writhing and praying. I have great joy always, and I have joy in watching what happens in my garden. But so often, there are questions, why? I don't deserve this, not ever able to make a future plan, just making it through each day, hour by hour, in prayer, claiming healing, begging for healing, realizing healing might not ever come, but holding onto God, devotedly, but accepting I had nothing else! So many of us don't want to be depressed, fight inwardly not to be, ashamed to be, but finally believing anyone with our lives would simply have to be! Try as I might, loving to read and study the sufferings of Paul in the Bible, I could not "consider it all joy." This disease is just the cruelest, seemingly, unending nightmare that I know. At lease with cancer, sometimes you "get" to die.

Continuing the Intervention Blocks

I continued with the intervention blocks. Sometimes there was short relief, some longer, never relieving the rectal pain. Dr. Reiheld was always looking for a better procedure, better relief. And, I continued on, being so afraid of my medication, breaking down, accepting that I must use them. All the while researching for any new treatment for myself and others. In July of 2016, hearing that a doctor was using an inter stimulator for pain relief, putting leads directly into the pudendal nerve, I quickly made plans to see him in Detroit. Surgeons never reopen entrapment surgery sites. My pain had increased drastically. I had no choice but to go see Dr. Michael Peters, a head of urology at Beaumont Health in Detroit who was doing this procedure. The trip progressed quickly. Dr. Peters was compassionate and found I was a candidate for the internal pain stimulator. Once again, hoping, praying this would at least bring some relief. I made two quick trips to Detroit. After the procedure, I was consumed by horrendous pain and burning across my entire buttocks and pelvic area. I was by myself with only an Uber driver to take me to the airport. He practically carried me in, finally finding a transport coordinator to take me through security. To board the plane, the flight attendant had to practically lift me into the plane and to my seat. I was absolutely helpless and consumed by pain. I had no choice but to lie against the sweet girl in the aisle seat. I arrived in Tampa out of my head with pain, unable to function. Thankfully, Ben got me home. This was just an awful recovery, the pain and burning never stopped. It felt as though my buttocks would just explode! Finally, returning for the follow up appointment, I was told I had many internal hematomas from placing the leads. They were drained and I eventually recovered from this procedure. I could turn the frequencies very high and shock my anal area to stop a major spasm! With this disease often comes the inability to have a bowel movement, trying brought on tremendous pain, so the shocking process of the inter-stimulator was somewhat effective for about two months. The end of believing I might get pain relief! I turned it off after three months, knowing it was not an answer and was of no use!

CHAPTER 9

Cherished Christmas

I continued on in my life of constant agony, from my bed to the lounger outside, trying to move and function when possible. Some relief came with the many blocks I was still having from my interventional radiologist. Such a precious group of professionals! These helped, but never eased the rectal spasms. At the Christmas 2016 worship service I was able to stand and greet at our church's huge "Christ" celebration. I love people and interaction, so it was a great joy to do this!

Preparing for a Trip to Meet Grandson

We were planning a trip after January 1st, 2017, to California to see our new 3-month-old grandson. I knew the long flight would be so difficult, but I wanted to hold Noah and my other two grands so badly. The Thursday night before we were to fly out on Monday, I had been in such constant agony. Finally, I collapsed with Ben grabbing me and holding me up. My body was in a full-blown attack once again. They are random, nothing brings them on. My husband, trying to help, told me I had to hang on as I said, "I just can't live through this!" so much agony, with my body ripping apart and every nerve quivering, blood pressure skyrocketing. I composed myself a bit to get to the bathroom, where I lay on the floor, demanding to know why God wouldn't let me die and how he could watch me like this. Hours passed like this, Ben giving me meds and compresses, begging me to drink liquor if he went for it. We don't buy or have it in our home. I did manage a giggle. I really didn't need to be drunk! I debated going to the Venice Emergency Room, but I was haunted by my underhanded lockup on the psych ward at Blount Memorial in Maryville Tennessee. We decided against it, fearing they wouldn't believe pudendal nerve pain as so many did not. Finally, the medication kicked in and I fell into a stupor and rested, at least for a few hours. Thank God I had an appointment the next day with interventional radiology for a previous whiplash.

Interventional Radiology to the Rescue

It was early morning Friday and we quickly got there. Normally, the nurses would bring me back quickly since I couldn't sit at all. When Dr. Reiheld came through, it was obvious as I lay in the fetal position, holding to the bars of the exam bed crying and unable to be still because of the high level of pain. He said #15 and I agreed! Unfortunately, I had to wait quite a while for the procedure room, since one hadn't been scheduled. But the doctor checked on me often. I had taken all the meds that I had, and nothing eased the pain. He is so kind, would take my hand, wishing he could make all the pain go away! He informed my husband that going to the ER the evening before would not have helped at all! But they did not have a psych ward if we had. Forgetting about treating the whiplash that I had made an appointment for, Dr. Reiheld said he would try different blocks on me that he had been researching. He asked if I could bear it without anesthesia, since he needed me to be awake for the trigger points. Assuring me if I could not bear the blocks that he would not do them if he thought they were too brutal! I went gladly to the procedure. I would have done anything to ease that attack. The needles were not pleasant, and there were many of them. In that state of pain, a person will do anything that might possibly bring relief! Horrible, but I lived through them. We were leaving in two days for California to see our new grandson, so with each injection of those huge, monster needles I knew they would hopefully enable me to make the flight.

Surviving the Trip to Meet Grandson

I had not flown anywhere in a couple of years and was surely not prepared for the long trip. It only took a short while to realize I was going to be in misery. After driving to Tampa, waiting at the terminal, a five-hour flight and then the two-hour ride up the coast near Santa Barbara. My son Brady is a Navy chaplain stationed there. The travel day lasted fourteen hours. On the flight, the fierce pain set in about 30 minutes after takeoff from Tampa. I had taken my normal meds, but soon knew they would not be sufficient. Always careful about taking more, I soon succumbed, knowing I was in trouble for this five-hour flight. I was in the seat on my knees, down on my knees in the floor, hanging onto the seat, twisting in total agony. I made it to California knowing that our visit with my son and his family probably would not be great fun. I put on a good face, truly thrilled to love on our two grands and baby Noah. My time that week was spent cuddling with the new baby, watching Ruby dress like a princess, helping her sing and making up very good stories for seven-year-old Lucius. Dreading the flight back across country, I had made my mind up – I would take as many oxys, pain suppositories, and relaxers as required to survive the flight! I did make it home still holding on to any strength I had to survive.

CHAPTER 10

Seeking Help

Before we had left Florida, I was making plans to fly back to St Paul, Minnesota to meet with Dr. Antolak. There had to be something we could discover to address my mounting pain, that had kept me bedfast for weeks. We flew to Minnesota four days after we returned home from California with the doctor's approval to take any meds necessary to get through the flight. He was giving us two full days, as he only comes in to his clinic for cases like mine. I hugged him, so thrilled he might discover a new reason for my pain. I knew he had saved my life once and would know what to do now. He truly is so compassionate and empathetic for all the suffering. We began early in the morning, exams, very carefully retracing nerves, and finding the worst pain locations. He is so brilliant as he traced from torso, spine to toes. Afternoons were spent at St. Joseph's hospital getting many blocks in my trigger points most reactive to pain. Two days were spent doing this, evaluating some nerves shooting pain went from hip, side to underneath the coccyx and rectal area. The culprit! And, once again, pointing back to my own 10-pound mangled breech birth. During one exam I said something that caused him to say "hmm...". One of my small toes on my left foot had been spasming with spike-like jabs for several months. He began to trace nerves up my left leg again, from foot to hip, leading him to the area to the left of my coccyx nearing my rectal area. For my adult life, I had been told I had sciatica. He informed me that I did not have sciatica! I was shocked but the toe problem made clear that other nerves were involved, shooting the radiating pain, butt pressure and great burning sensation and horrific feeling that my coccyx was constantly being pulled out.

Seeking Specialized Care

Dr. Reiheld, my interventional radiologist, and Dr. Antolak consulted. He agreed to epidurals with several infusions of pain killers, numbing medicines and steroids. Leaving Minnesota with a plan, I felt as though the pain blocks had a specific target. He also wanted steady epidural infusions every two weeks for three months. Dr. Reiheld was always willing to do any new procedure that might help me! The epidurals were painful, not just an epidural shot, but placing the needle and infusing by catheter to several areas, pain relieving concoctions throughout my spine and hopefully the offending nerves. Some gave relief more than others, but none ever affected the rectal spasms! It is such an area of many nerves, obviously a difficult area to affect one single nerve. We gladly went to the nearby office twice weekly, now using steroids and other concoctions each time for three months. By June 2017 I knew the epidural route was not relieving the horrific pain.

A Potential Lead

Around that time, I had a sweet friend who happened to be prowling in her local library and picked up a random newspaper, overjoyed at an article she found. She called, so excited, telling me of the article and a doctor's interview, stated his qualifications, a colorectal surgeon, who also specialized in pudendal nerve issues. So, I thought this was a sign from God, since my friend never goes to the library and just happened to pick an old newspaper. Another quest began! I got an appointment to see him, so excited that I had found a specialist nearby. My husband and I had searched since the summer of 2015 for any specialist in pudendal nerve disease, never finding, and never ending the search!

CHAPTER 11

Disappointment with the Colorectal Surgeon

The first visit with this doctor began with just a few questions and a quick rectal exam, sending me screaming on the table with knife stabbing pain, taking a while to recover from a very painful assault on the nerves. We set an appointment for the second of July 2016 for the inter-stim to be removed, in order to have new MRIs. I thought the removal was three weeks later. I checked in and was having to remind the doctor why I was there and that the inter-stim had to be removed. I was told I had to talk with the representative from Medtronic, the maker of the unit before he could proceed. Frustrated, I left after five minutes. I waited for the representative to call, I had no clue who to call. Into the third week, I called the doctor's office to inquire why I hadn't been contacted. I was then told that I was supposed to contact the representative myself. Then she was on vacation for two weeks. After three more weeks, I called the rep, leaving message after message. Finally getting a call, she informed me, it was my choice to remove the unit, and that she was not to be involved! After two more weeks, the doctor finally set up the removal. Never seeing or speaking to him, I had no idea how to proceed. Two more weeks passed, and I had a follow-up appointment. Briefly, he walked in and asked how I was and smiled as if removing the inter stimulator had cured me. I answered, "I'm horrible!" Three minutes in the exam room he told me the next step was eight months of biofeedback. I stared in disbelief and let him know biofeedback would do nothing for this pain! He snapped that he was the expert, and this was the next step. I don't remember what I said, but unable not to weep, I begged him to help! "What do you want me to do," he asked. I yelled that I wanted him to go in and get the nerve that he touched that sent me into agony. He left the room. Eventually, I got to the front desk where eight months of biofeedback had been scheduled. I couldn't control myself. I wept, not cried, unable to leave the office. I had put so much hope in the surgeon who had wasted so many months of my time and my life! The nurses consoled me with, "I understand. I know, I know." Irritated, I yelled back through tears, "NO, you don't! You couldn't unless you were delivering a baby and your tailbone was being jerked out!" Finally, collecting myself, I made it through the office, weeping as I went to my car. You notice no one when gripped in pain! I sat out front for at least an hour, calling my daughter-in-law, who's easy to talk to. I told her I was sure God wanted me to die! Otherwise, why would all the doctor visits, the seemingly Godinspired direction to each specialist, then always, always no success, no help, no pain relief at all. We talked, she assured me, soothed me somewhat and I was able to leave the doctor's parking lot. I only got as far as the huge tree in a mall across the street. I could not stop the shock, trembling and uncontrollably weeping. After quite a while, I decided I had to call Dr. Antolak in Minnesota. So thankful he answered, I could only get a few words out about the disappointment, asking, "how can I possibly live through this disease any longer?" He told me to come to Minnesota immediately and he would treat me all summer. He had success in repeat procedures. I didn't know of all he would do, but I had his promise to help. We probably talked an hour, he soothed and consoled me, so we decided that would be my option. It's easy to understand how I adore him and will be forever indebted to him. I made one more call to Lyndsey, the nurse to Dr. Reiheld, my interventional radiologist. She could hardly understand the message I left in my emotional state. I just wanted Dr. Reiheld to block the pain! Finally, I felt I could compose myself enough to drive home. It seemed at times my husband would have to come to the so-called specialist's office to pick me up. I got through the nineteen miles back to Venice, in great pain. Having an idea to just drop into my husband's colorectal surgeon to beg, plead, whatever it took for one of the surgeons to see me. I was somewhat out of my head. At the front desk, I tried to make the staff understand, I simply was dying. A nurse took me inside. I tried to explain to her what pudendal nerve disease was. Of course, she had never heard the word! I was once again bent over in horrendous pain and weeping. She agreed to go into the head doctor's office, explain my plight and beg him to see me. He agreed to see me one week later, not helping me at the moment, but I was thankful he would at least consider listening. I wanted everything out, of course not knowing what everything was! Just rid my body of the "Monster". As I left that office, Lyndsey, Dr. Reiheld's nurse, called me. She had gleaned from my broken words what had happened. She had talked to the doctor who knew the unfathomable pain an attack brought on. His advice was to stop any searching for specialists in Venice or the surrounding cities. He said to start searching in Tampa or Miami for a highly qualified neurologist. This is what he would have his own wife do if she was in my situation.

Searching for Neurological Expertise

So once again, the search began. We were now looking for neurosurgeons. Ben and I, when able, were constantly online searching for a surgeon. We contacted University of South Florida at Tampa, University of Miami Hospital, Mayo in Miami, and Johns Hopkins Hospital at Jacksonville. All of these except Johns Hopkins said they had no pelvic pain unit. After many phone transfers at Johns Hopkins, I reached the proper department for pudendal nerve disease, the neuro surgery department. After giving much information at every transfer, I reached this department only to be told they were booked with seeing patients almost two years in advance. This was hopeless. I would not live two years! Finally, I reached the highest recognized neurosurgeon at University of Miami Hospital. Surprised, I was seen in one week on a Saturday. He hardly introduced himself, but he was brilliant, and this was all I needed. He studied my new, lower abdomen pelvic MRI and wanted to see my older MRIs also. Seemingly, so interested, he pointed out spots, curves, some stenosis, a serious bend of my vertebrae at my neck, saying, "The pain could be generated from so many of these places." I had to remain standing and wiggling constantly from the pain. It seemed so promising that he would treat me! He wanted new MRIs of the entire spine and set me up for an appointment the next Friday. Talking as though he would send me directly to the University of Miami Medical center.

The Search for Help Continues

I moved heaven and earth to get all new MRIs that week. Anxious, we left Venice Friday with such high hopes. After all, he had seemed so shocked seeing my nerves and crooked spine. We got to his office at 9 a.m. full of hope. After all, he knew my nerves and talked as though he was ready to help! I got into the exam room. The nurse had popped up all the new MRIs. He walked into the room, not saying one word. He may have glanced at the MRIs, I think not, and immediately said "I can't help you." I was shocked, standing, unable to sit or lie. I just stared in disbelief. I asked what I was supposed to do with a tailbone seemingly being ripped from my body and deathly pain that was constant. Always! He calmly said, "I can't help you; I can give you an injection." And he walked out. This very expensive appointment, probably $700 because of his expertise and title, was no longer than three minutes. Sometime during the week, he had decided he just wasn't going to take me as a patient.

Setbacks and Continued Searching

We headed back to Venice, broken! Again! I had contacted another neurosurgeon who listed pudendal nerve disease as a specialty. I called repeatedly for four weeks only to find he had left orders, weeks earlier to send me to Dr. Aaron Fuller in Maryland, who had retired years before. Another Miami surgeon, who had very little interest in helping a desperate human! By mid-May, I was grappling with how I could survive. Ben and I were constantly on social media searching for any help in Florida, South Carolina and North Carolina. Repeatedly hearing every day, "no help," "we don't do that." No professional could recommend anyone, anywhere. Now we searched for any specialist, who at least, did internal pain blocks, vaginally under anesthesia. I knew they had literally saved my life in 2009 in Chattanooga. Not one specialist we found did these in the three states we were looking in, so hard to believe, but true. I had decided if I got these blocks, I could at least live a while longer. My husband and I searched day and night, calling constantly, this bringing on so much stress. Every morning, after my God time, I began the hunt again. So, so many disappointments. At times there was just no one left to google, no searches left, having to accept there was just no one. Knowing I could have always gone to Minnesota to Dr. Antolak, the pudendal nerve "missionary," but, not wanting to spend the summer of 2017 in a motel, I was about to accept that plan was probably the only plan! Along with this, trying to live through the level-15 pain attacks (yes, they can always be a level 15). Battling these attacks were constant, caught up in such horror, weeping constantly, not crying, trying not to wear the pain on my face and forever pleading with God to please release me, let me die, blood pressure soaring, heart racing, internal tremors from head to toe, uncontrollable shaking, grabbing the hard medications that seemingly took forever to ease just a tiny bit of pain, never reaching to the tailbone seemingly being pulled out. I would weep and beg for God to see me, give mercy, let me go, to no avail! This, I will never understand! Being a faithful, lifetime Christian, I know He could hear, making the pain all disappear in an instant. I have raged, that I didn't deserve this most awful disease! I literally battled God!

CHAPTER 12

A Glimmer of Hope in Chattanooga

Once again, one morning in mid-June as Ben and I were searching for help for myself and a suffering, young single mother in North Carolina with similar symptoms (One must try to help another when you know and feel their agony) the name of Dr. Furr in Chattanooga ran through my mind. I remembered at one time seven years ago when I was seeing Dr. Nieves, Dr. Furr was training to do the internal blocks. Dr. Furr received his degrees abroad and did his residency in obstetrics and gynecology at Loyola Medical Center in Chicago. He had completed a study in advanced minimally invasive surgery with Dr Cy Liu. His practice was now focused on pelvic pain management. I found him online and called immediately. I told his surgical scheduler I knew he did blocks but asked if they knew anyone in middle Tennessee or surrounding areas who had learned pudendal nerve surgery. "Oh, Dr. Furr does that now," she said. I just dropped the phone, burst out in heart ripping sobs, unable to talk. Thankfully, Ben was sitting by to take the phone. In a few minutes, still crying, I told her my situation and asked how soon he could see me. Sadly, she said he was booked into next year. Weeping again, I told her I wouldn't make it, stating horrible details. She found someone to talk to and asked if I could fly the next day, Tuesday, and he would see me Wednesday morning. Absolutely, no question, I would be there! We raced to Tampa,

I flew to Knoxville, and drove to Maryville, "home" with my sister ready to get me to Chattanooga at 9 a.m. Wednesday. She had driven me there many times after 2009 to Dr. Nieves. Chattanooga was only a two-hour drive, and we arrived at his office sharply at 9am.

Finally, a Doctor Willing to Help

With almost no wait, not nervous at all, one isn't when they've gone through such painful battles, and, so grateful since our other surgeons will never revisit or look at pudendal entrapment surgery a second time. Dr. Furr looked at me, as I was unable to sit or lie, holding on to the exam table, shaking. He quickly asked if I wanted him to increase my medications. I questioned since even narcotics had not helped in the last three months. I know he saw the agony on my face! He said he would not examine me in my condition, "wouldn't put me through that." I was so thankful, since the exam brings on spasms that mimic childbirth! He would wait until I was under anesthesia to do the exam. He proceeded to write prescriptions for stronger, pure oxycodone and an internal numbing cream. I was to come back the following Monday, July 19, 2017, for exploratory surgery where the pudendal nerve and surrounding pelvic area, rectal and coccyx pain would be investigated. I would have begged to stay for sooner treatment, but I was so thankful that he had been kind, compassionate and understanding. With new medication, I felt I could survive another week.

Preparing for Surgery

It was a difficult week. The new, stronger medication, along with drug combinations in the suppositories Dr. Antolak had prescribed, eased the pain for a few hours each time. I confess now, that I really didn't worry about the number of narcotics I had to take. I needed to survive until my surgery! The time between my first visit to Dr. Furr and my surgery date was spent at my sister's house near Knoxville. I had put together an area in her garden with a large padded swing, big box fan, going on full blast toward my face, and of course my inspirational, encouraging music. This was all to distract me from the constant pain, listening to the song birds in large trees "cocooning" around me, shooing at new bunnies nibbling on fresh summery flowers and watching family come and go. It was somewhat helpful at letting my mind intermittently think of what was happening all around. "Early in the morning I will arise and seek your face" has been a guiding Bible verse for me. Doing this was easy for me as sleep evaded me. With medication, I would drift off in the early hours of morning and pop totally awake most mornings before sunrise. Many hours of sleep would have been such a blessing since that was the only time I didn't realize the ever-present pain. Reading these things, I know is incredulous. So many, many people would say, "just close your eyes and sleep!" To an insomniac, whose mind simply does not stop thinking, this is such a cruel comment. I had suffered extreme insomnia since February 1985 and had no prescriptions or procedures that were effective for sleep at all until January 1988. Thank God for a psychiatrist who demanded I start an anti-anxiety drug. I resisted, insisting that I had nothing to be anxious about other than needing sleep! But I was so grateful as I began to drift off at night. Insomnia, for me, was a familial abnormality, stemming from no event or incident. Also, in my case, there was no such thing as napping, ever, no matter how tired or run down I was. Looking back, I am amazed that I could function for three years, perfect home, wife, and mother, telling no one except my husband. No one would believe any way that sleep simply would not come. I continued, in a stupor, mind confused day and night, so weary and worn. My thought was, "One

Continuing the Search for Relief

The original plan from Dr. Furr was to be in Chattanooga for surgery in 5-7 weeks. I had new, stronger medication being pure oxycontin, 20 mg, not altered with Tylenol, and new vaginal numbing cream, along with my anal suppositories, the combination of four pain drugs with anti-spasmodic medications. Finishing the tube of vaginal cream, expensive and not covered by insurance, I decided to discontinue usage as my pain was not vaginal. I had presumed I could wait for treatment for the few weeks, realizing the wait was impossible! The initial blocks soon were totally ineffective!

The Return of Excruciating Pain

One week after this procedure my pain was back with a vengeance! After a few short hours of sleep, I awakened with the familiar stabbing, contracting spasms. As these grew in intensity, the pain radiated into the large sacral bone, "the sit bones" (doctor to patient vernacular) and the vaginal area, spreading downward. This is so hard to explain, such an all-encompassing area. The drugs became useless, unrelenting pain started early in the morning, ending only if I could fall asleep. I lay outside on the swing, pacing the yard, trying so hard to occupy my mind with any distraction. I would stare into the sky, asking God for peace in my acceptance of this once-again returned stage of my illness.

Contemplating the Unthinkable

By the end of the week, I had determined that I simply could not live on! After bouts of stealing away to my dark room, on my face in prayer so many times, giving into the peace of ending it all seemed totally logical. Nothing else could be done to help me. After all, this war had been going on for eleven years. Had I not grasped at every hope of medical and God-given help? Exhausting all, this time had decidedly come. One last ditch effort. In that dark bedroom, I had wept and prayed until my face was swollen, I willed myself to make one more call to the surgeon's office.

CHAPTER 13

A Whisper of Hopefulness

previous call that week, speaking to the nurses benefited nothing. This time I would speak only to Dr. Furr's scheduler, Thursday being her last day of the week. Barely coherent, I told Emily my situation. She said, "Let me find someone to talk to." In the background I heard the doctor say, "tell her she won't have to wait five to seven weeks, I'm going to work her in." I rested upon hearing that. "Maybe, I can make it!" My husband flew into Knoxville immediately. We quickly started for Chattanooga with my surgery scheduled for July 19th.

Surgery Without Fear

There is no fear or anxiety awaiting surgery when it's your only lifeline! I didn't fear anything. I had already faced death repeatedly and actually longed for its respite! Such are the thoughts of one living with severe chronic pain! I've had a few surgeries and many times I would stress and worry as the time slowly arrived, so upset at the thought of what ifs, death, cancer, ineptitude of the surgeons. But those thoughts are long gone, especially as I waited for my extensive and complicated surgery with Dr. Furr, so grateful that a doctor was agreeing to look inside my tormented body!

Unexpected Findings and Extensive Surgery

Dr. Furr and I had a short talk before the surgery. I told him I was in his hands and God's. He had my permission to do anything he thought would benefit me. Off we went. In total surrender I prayed for God to guide the doctor's hands, but if He would allow, I was ready to come home and end my nightmare. Surgery began around 11 a.m. but stopped abruptly. Dr. Furr came out to talk with Ben informing him I was covered with endometriosis. "Shocking", the doctor said, "This is killing her!" And he asked permission to do extensive surgery. "Of course, do whatever you need to do," was Ben's reply.

Agonizing Recovery

What a surprise! I had a hysterectomy in 2007 and didn't know one could have endometriosis afterwards. Dr. Furr still says he has never seen any as bad. Thank God, the doctor was doing laparoscopic surgery, or this disease would never have been seen. Along with the pudendal neuralgia and the nerves shooting from my coccyx and down my leg, there is absolutely no question that I know I couldn't have lived two more weeks. The internal pictures we were given show so much area of lasered flesh, extensively under my ribs, growing upward and wrapped around my rectum. I have told the doctor, "Don't rush the endometrial patients out of the hospital." There was great anguish driving back to my sister's house near Knoxville. For over one week I couldn't twist my body or straighten. I finally got out of the bed to go to the bathroom, and it took all the strength I had.

Temporary Relief and Renewed Hope

I was given necessary pain meds as I recuperated. I had no choice but to be immobile, so I lay under the trees in the garden as much as possible. It's a horrible thing to have been such an active person for years then having to accept that part of my life would never come again. But I had my music, Bible, and birds to sing, so time passed on. By August I was back in Venice, Florida. I would love to write here that surgery had been a total success and my body had been rid of endometriosis and the pudendal nerve "Monster" had been conquered. It only took a short time in July to realize that wasn't the case. I survived with medication until mid-September to do my re-check with the doctor. Once again, I longed for time to pass in order to have the internal blocks again. Thank God these are drugs that can be used sooner than every three months! Dr. Furr has been so willing to do anything possible to alleviate or lessen the pain. He truly is a Godsend!

Thanksgiving and Christmas of 2017

This Thanksgiving and Christmas of 2017 really had no happy memories or celebrations. There were no wonderful, Southern, massive feasts. We actually had sandwiches. This broke my heart and drove the realization deeper that my life as I had known it was over. I describe myself as one who gets giddy over these two holidays. Growing up we were very poor but were always able to share these meals that made the holidays special. Giddy also for the many blessings, but also for my Savior, who has kept me all my life! Even in all the career years away from my huge family, we made Christmas the most glorious holiday, never forgetting its true meaning, and also being able to search and provide that gift so perfect for extended family and our children, Leigh and Brady. Then the joy of our grandchildren, we have six, ages 21 to 2 years. I don't believe one can truly appreciate this feeling unless they've lived a time of not being able financially to give. I want nothing, have all I've needed, but Lord, please let me give! There had been no festive shopping, unable to get out of bed, my "babies" received gifts ordered online.

A Cherished Bright Spot in the Season

Once again, I was in Tennessee in mid-December. And at church there was a cherished bright spot in the season. Having just had my many blocks in Chattanooga, I contacted my very special friend and choir director, asking if I could sing in the concerts. "Of course!" I had always memorized every line, so quickly, I got busy! Choir and my church had been my lifeline in the eight years we lived in Maryville, never wearing my pain on my face, I worshipped in total abandonment!

CHAPTER 14

Preparing for Surgery

Traveling back to Florida before Christmas day, I prepared for a flight back to see Dr. Furr for the repeat surgery I was promised on January 10th, 2018. Of course, I prayed for and expected this to finally reveal the culprit of my nightmare. The doctor and I talked before surgery as I begged him to search nerves throughout and into my hips and left leg. "Please do anything you see that might help!" Always compassionate, he promised he would do all he could, but he couldn't promise what the results would be. I had peace. I had nothing except the power of God and the surgeon He provided.

Waiting for Life-Extending Blocks

In mid-March 2018, once again, I waited in Tennessee for my life extending blocks. They had for many months stopped being effective at all, realized as quickly as I awaken from procedures. For the last few weeks, Dr. Furr had been using a new drug, hoping to build us some sort of long-lived relief. I let him know that I must have anything for some pain relief! I have strong meds. I can't seem to write or say since they seem not to help the pain any longer! I bear the stigma of being a drug user. Self-inflicted as my doctors have been adamant that I use them all. I succumbed months ago. I would be blessed to sleep all day, but the drugs make me hyper. My night sleep is often three hours or less. I know my body needs rest, and I have sedatives but also familial insomnia. I write now that I have no clue of what the next hour might bring except pain. There is no plan for tomorrow or any future. A few weeks ago, I stopped praying for and claiming healing. God has provided miracles at times. There can be no other explanations. I don't believe in coincidence.

The Pain Pump and Seeking Relief

In October 2020 I allowed an intrathecal pain pump to be installed by my pain management doctor, Gregory Ball. As of this date after many trials and adjustments, I have had no benefit from the device. In April of this year, Dr. Furr did laparoscopic surgery to move a lead directly to the pudendal nerve. As the pain pump slowly empties itself of pain medication, Dr. Ball is now refilling the pump with Bupivacaine, a local anesthetic. If only this will reach my spasmodic anal canal, which is an everyday battle with almost no medications except pain suppositories. These do not take a bit of the pain away. However, I am still bedfast and have only been out to doctor's appointments, not even to my beloved choir or church, which kept me alive and surviving.

Facing 14 Years of Pudendal Nerve Damage

It is May 2021. I can hardly say which birthday it is, but I am thankful to have another birthday this month. Also, this June makes my nightmare with pudendal nerve damage 14 years long. It is hard to believe the years, but despite many procedures and several surgeries, I am still suffering. I do say the most beneficial surgery I've had was with Dr. Robert Furr, my amazing specialist in Chattanooga TN. He had studied and researched the removal of half the pudendal nerve, mine being the right side. I can absolutely say this surgery in June 2020 has helped rid my pain much as the original bilateral surgery with

Dr. Antolak in Minnesota. Sadly, since that original surgery, I have kept developing scar tissue. At that time, I had six months of blessed relief before the pain returned. With Dr. Furr removing the right pudendal, the ripping pain similar to labor pains has subsided. Sweet relief, if only my rectal spasms and sit bone pain could be removed.

CHAPTER 15

Surviving and Pressing On

For whatever reason, my body is prone to creating scar tissue, which is bringing back my battle with the pain. I have prayed for healing constantly and fervently! There has been no answer to end my suffering. I have survived incredibly. I only know I would not have without the provision of brilliant doctors and Dr. Furr, who has always thought of another procedure that might help me. In the mornings now, whether it is 3 a.m., dark or moon glowing, if I've had a longer respite (I don't feel pain if I sleep), I look out full glass doors from bed. My first words are "Thank you Lord, for your beauty! And, secondly, Father God, just help me live through the pain today, wrap me in mercy!" After many years of this battle, from June 2007 till now, I long for healing and life again, knowing it may not come. I press on in my battle to survive!

I pray this simple writing might give hope, not disappointment to the sufferers. There are dedicated doctors for this disease and help is available for so, so many. I would never want anyone reading this to think that Pudendal nerve disease is a death sentence. Thousands upon thousands have had surgeries releasing the nerve from entrapment successfully. As I've said in an after-surgery video on YouTube, it is mostly a noncomplicated surgery with very little pain or complications afterwards. Some people have worries and concerns because the surgery sounds awful, and they avoid surgery out of fear. So many have thanked me for encouraging them to follow through with the surgery. If you are one of these sufferers, there is no need to be without hope. Our amazing doctors can give you your life back. Many sufferers can have a full and wonderful life!

CHAPTER 16

The Greatest Suffering

My life has been a tumultuous roller-coaster of emotions, and I am sharing this journey with the world for a singular purpose: to encourage those facing adversity that they can endure their trials. While my struggles have been primarily physical in nature, I recognize that many in this world also grapple with emotional, mental health, and relational pains. Some must bear the anguish of losing a beloved father, mother, son, or daughter. Others suffer the debilitating effects of anxiety and depression. And in certain parts of the globe, individuals and families are forced to endure the cruel realities of financial hardship, hunger, and lack of economic support - unable to even provide their children with basic sustenance for daily life.

We all have our own personal battles to face, and I believe this is simply an inescapable part of the human experience. But one thing is certain: these pains serve as reminders that life in this world is far from perfect. This earthly realm is merely a temporary dwelling, and there exists a flawless, eternal place that God, through His Son Jesus Christ, has reserved for us - the suffering souls. As it is written in Revelation 21:4 (NASB), "He will wipe away every tear from their eyes; and there will no longer be any death; there will no longer be any mourning, or crying, or pain; the first things have passed away." I cling to this promise of a promised land where God will bestow His grace upon each and every one of us.

These trials we endure in life are ultimately tests of our faith in Him. Day by day, we encounter new sources of pain and anguish. But all we must do is surrender those burdens to the Lord and seek to understand the purpose behind our suffering. As human beings, we are often tempted to question God when we find ourselves in the throes of adversity, asking, "Have I not been a good person?" or "Have I not lived my life according to God's will?" The answer, however, is simple: these pains are opportunities to strengthen our reliance on the Lord's promises. Do we truly trust in His unwavering support when we are engulfed by pain and suffering? Or do we succumb to the temptation of blaming God for our circumstances? How resolute is our faith in the face of life's most daunting challenges?

Let us not forget that the scriptures have already forewarned us: Christians can expect to encounter "many troubles" - be they mental, physical, emotional, or spiritual in nature (Psalm 34:19). It is also written that all followers of Christ will suffer (John 16:33; Acts 14:22). The Apostle Paul himself experienced a myriad of hardships (as documented in 2 Corinthians 4:8-10), and the disciples of Christ were no strangers to suffering.

Yet, we must remember that no matter the severity of our own afflictions, they pale in comparison to the unimaginable torment endured by Jesus Christ. He was mocked, whipped, his bones chilled in agony, his wrists and feet pierced, his very frame dislocated as he suffered the ultimate torment on the cross. All of this, so that he could wash away our sins and iniquities, and provide us the precious gift of eternal life, if only we believe. He bore the weight of the world's transgressions, past, present, and future, because God the Father so loved the world (John 3:16).

So I challenge my readers: How does your pain measure up to the unfathomable suffering Jesus experienced on the cross of Calvary? As fallible human beings, are we truly willing to endure the kind of anguish the Savior willingly accepted for our sake?

I doubt it. But know this: our earthly tribulations can only be healed when we place our unwavering trust in Him. There have been numerous occasions in my life where I have given up all hope, only for God to call me back to the fight, reminding me never to surrender, for these are tests of faith. I am far from perfect, and I have certainly voiced my complaints to the Lord. But in the end, I have come to the realization that the pain Jesus bore on the cross for me is incomparable to any of my own suffering. With that revelation, I find solace in the knowledge that after all my trials and tribulations, I will one day be reunited with my Savior in the heavenly realm, where tears, pain, and trouble will be no more.

Author's Biography

I'm definitely a country girl and proud of it. However, with my husband's job with JC Penney Co., we had moved from one side of the country to the other, seeing much and learning to meet people from all locations in the world. We had a great time showing our two children some wonderful sights in the amazing country!

I love all the people, but nothing has impressed me more that the upbringing I had in our small country area outside of Maryville, TN. I credit my mother. Studying every afternoon was her lifeline. She told us many times over how the Bible would have us live. This is my most cherished memory and certainly has attributed to the person I am today, not perfect, but always forgiven.

www.ingramcontent.com/pod-product-compliance
Lightning Source LLC
Chambersburg PA
CBHW070938120626
46546CB00004B/1457